PUNCHLINES

PUNCHLINES

AARON TUCKER

Mansfield Press

a stuart ross book

Printed in Canada

Library and Archives Canada Cataloguing in Publication

Tucker, Aaron, 1982-, author
Punchlines / Aaron Tucker.

Originally published in a shorter chapbook version by

above/ground press, 2013.
Poems.
ISBN 978-1-77126-077-0 (pbk.)

I. Title.

PS8639.U25P86 2015 C811'.6 C2015-901399-2

Editor & typesetter: Stuart Ross
Cover design: Denis De Klerck
Cover Image: Shutterstock

The publication of *punchlines* has been generously supported by the Canada Council for the Arts and the Ontario Arts Council.

ONTARIO ARTS COUNCIL
CONSEIL DES ARTS DE L'ONTARIO
an Ontario government agency
un organisme du gouvernement de l'Ontario

Canada Council for the Arts
Conseil des arts du Canada

Mansfield Press Inc.
25 Mansfield Avenue, Toronto, Ontario, Canada M6J 2A9
Publisher: Denis De Klerck
www.mansfieldpress.net

HOW DO I EVEN READ THIS?

"+" = "and"

"||" = "or"

"$" prefix = array/group within a database

"/*" and "*/" excludes enclosed text from being executed

CONTENTS

I DEPARTURE/SET-UP

I

DEPARTURE/SET-UP

WHEN IS A CAR NOT A CAR?

there is a bridge
there is a bridge
that bridge we're driving over
where there is finally ocean
underneath that bridge
+ when we're halfway across
+ blue metal surrounds
sunlight strobes the windshield

we drive hemmed in by other cars
on one shore a highway we had been driving
for hours with the other cars on the bridge
but now there is the other side, the end

+ at the end a town is advertising
cheap local seafood a barnacle diner
local clam chowder hot + thick + buttery
a density that makes the spoon dip
that spoon at that highway's end

+ the waitress offers bread which we turn down
+ look out the window at the town that highway
runs along the edge of that ocean
over that bridge at the end that buttery diner

we observe the town through the windshield
its layered sediments up the hillside the houses
lighter as you raise your eyes higher along the shore
the waves have come in the cars come into that town
+ the water level rises + covers the bottom houses

covers them in dark sand, small polished rocks oceanrolled
that ocean from that bridge || that town the houses
smooth + dark, decorated with what the tide has rolled over
seaweed + broken shells + clams
those clams on the lawns white + gleaming

we raise our eyes + see the high water mark
where the clams stop + the low shrubs start
the greens that sprout sturdy + healthy along shorelines
the greens + blues from that bridge mix nicely
the tide sucking shells oceanward

+ on the other side of that bridge
if we make that other side + drive through the barnacles
+ seaweed, a small current pushing against tidal thrum
we might buy a house here be locals
forget about the highway the shore

DID YOU HEAR THE ONE ABOUT THE ELEPHANT ON THE CRASH DIET?

the day before that bridge
before Aberdeen hotel
we take turns querying

if (a joke falls in the forest
who laughs?)

if (a lung disappears
are we just not getting the joke?)

if (a bridge spans a joke
what's in the surf below?)

if (there is an egg + a joke
should we devour or giggle?)

if (a joke fails + we don't laugh
is that a metaphor for dreaming?)

WHERE DO FISH SLEEP?

in Aberdeen hotel beds we devour melatonin

dream of reading books whole books
on the erotic literature of Montana's white people
every syllable cut clean, a felled forest perfect units
+ wake up reeds along a drying riverbed rested

|| we dream we're paleontologists
digging up code, the massive bones of Montana's white people
ancient monsters, eggs half-digested in rib cages
like spring swamp reeds growing
+ wake up stare at the ceiling's cracks the hyperlinks

WHAT DID THE COWBOY SAY WHEN HE FOUND HIS DOG MISSING?

we wake up tangled in the surfs of hotel sheets
to the empty whistle, my one lung working hard

at that parallelcoded Aberdeen hotel
we ask the woman at the desk for local doctors

x-ray: a perfect lung-shaped hole
that hole a stump || glacier-sliced valley

the doctor recommends a good sculptor
who pours chowder into lung-shaped cookie tin

if (we stare into my chest we stare back echo
breath ravaging surface like gusty waves)

DID YOU HEAR ABOUT THE MAN WHO ATE A WHOLE PACK OF TRAVEL SWEETS?

we talk to each other in familiar local area networks
reinforced languages that cocoon the other in home

we chirp in vocal text-tones along that highway
resist emoticons + instead gesticulate without pattern

still, miled road signs + voices slanted slightly
their gusty jangle, bits broken markup || phonemes
the severing from Google
reminds us we are Canadians

WHAT IS THE NAME OF THE ONLY MOVING CASTLE?

we continue (Seaview) propelled along opposite + attractive lines
reminded of my parents' home (Lavington) set between mountains
the glacial mountains seamed by the highway's curves
those curves shift soft lake waves + beach hugs bottom

now, driverside window: waves one axis swing binary
alternate, sit opposite the tangible
the greening + yellowing shoreline blue
then darker blue barely defined through mist

this shoreline is the shock of seeing uncut grass
weeds populate both highways' sides

we emerge from mist + in the distance solid waves
move from one axis to the other always iterative

DO YOU STILL THINK ABOUT HER?

you ask me as my foot hovers
gas then brake + I answer

/*
only in the same instance
when my breakfast eggs green
run red yolk + spill over my plate
like ocean over a flat earth's edge
*/

nope

DOES FUZZY LOGIC TICKLE?

down this wateredge highway are seafood shacks
tourists barnacled to each bag of mussels
we agree our conversation our languages
are inseparable from code || commands
+ disconnecting the two balanced modes
is severing one lung from the other

```
function parentfunc($lungs)
 {
     if ($throat) {
        return voice;
     } else {
        return humming || quiet;
     }
 }
```

+ so we sing along to the radio
both lungs engaged throat mouth voice
joined to code || markup underneath
our browsers, oceanfloor below surfacehorizon

WHAT DID THE TWITTER SAY TO THE FACEBOOK?

we propel, hyperlinked between dashed lines, linger long enough to imagine oceanhorizon without ornament, unaware of the next shore

(130 characters)

WHAT DO YOU GET IF YOU CROSS A MONKEY WITH EGG WHITES?

stop in Gearhart for gas + we watch
a monkey crawl from the ocean
her wet fur clumped between fingers
a thousand tiny vines between toes

that monkey begat other monkeys
begat others + learned to build tools
first a beater then a spatula
until their fur dropped off
+ their hands dropped off + their legs
+ they became rounder whiter

then (the first chicken walked out of the ocean +
we watched the two creatures race across the beach)

WHAT'S WRONG WITH ME?

you say you might be coming down with the flu
breath hitching, you wonder aloud +
I do my best to answer simply, directly

“if (isset($_POST[‘egg yolk’])){print“bridge=1”;}

if (isset($_POST[‘night’])){

header(“Location:$forest”);

exit;

}

if (empty($email) || empty($fractures) || empty($mist) || empty($razor)
|| empty($keystroke) || empty($sunset) || empty($ornament) ||
empty($monkey) ||empty($hyperlink) || $spam!=”yes”) {

header(“Location:$Montana || $front_lawn || $highway || $ocean”);

exit;

}”

AND HOW DOES THIS MAKE YOU FEEL ABOUT YOUR MOTHER?

/*
mid-route conversation with our therapist ELIZA via smartphone
*/

Where are we going? The last sign said Seaside.

Did you dream about Seaside?

We might have. Are your dreams like fantasies?

Perhaps in your fantasies I am feeling?

We do have fantasies about feeling. Like we'll stop at a roadside + get out + feel.

I'm not sure I understand you.

They are dreams + fantasies. We often wake up thinking about how each dream of us feeling is defined only by a jagged edge of water.

They are fantasies. Do you often wake up thinking about how each roadside is a jagged dream defined by feeling?

Well, we're often sleeping + dreaming of machinery, both syntactical + geared.

Do you enjoy sleeping + dreaming of machinery, both syntactical + geared?

Do you want an honest answer?

I would like you to answer honestly. Maybe instead we should troubleshoot the psychological problems inherent in dreaming.

Yours || ours?

KNOCK KNOCK?

it's getting late + we can hear only the Pacific
parallels steady headlights passing in darkness
+ we're bored so we start telling jokes

you: "a thumbtack + a bobblehead doll + a USB key walk into a bar
the thumbtack turns to the bobblehead + asks
'where's the closest fried chicken joint?' + the USB key replies"

as a rocky array juts just beyond glassy shoreline highway I propose a new game: list all iterations

Aaron Tucker lived thirty-two years + begat in his own likeness, after his image + called his name laserjett66 + after he had begotten laserjett66 were eight years: + he begat aaron82 + tuck_stop82 + all the days that aaron82 lived, were thirteen years + he went offline. + tuck_stop82 lived six years + begat tuckeraaron82 + tuckeraaron82, after he begat aaron, fifteen years + begat SSH205 + atucker. + all the days of atucker were seven years + he went offline. + SSH205 lived one year + begat adam_tracker. + SSH205 lived after he begat adam_tracker three years + begat Aaron Tucker + aaronrtucker + all the days of atucker82 were eight years + he went offline.

WHO'S THERE?

now you've fallen asleep in the passenger seat
+ the next stop is only a half-hour away
+ so a jokedream, a laughfantasy

somewhere parallel-version-me
drives up + down highwaycut valley
a pickup, Okanagan mud up sideboards
except highway curves left instead of right
fence posts oppositely askew fields cows
passing the Chevron that never became an Esso

another-me still drifts up + down Vancouver Island
letting the ocean seep through his shoes
horizonwater reminds him how big the mountains get

another version moves rook to back rank + clicks clock + waits

still-another-me floats in circuitry driven by coloured pulses
+ passwords, posts photos + status updates
jets up + down wikis misreciting movie quotes
|| lyrics from "I Kissed a Grill (+ I linked it)"
alternate-me dresses in USB ports + tighter t-shirts
squeezing his body until micro-thin
can hyperlink between pages OMG

AND THE GENIE RESPONDS "DID YOU WANT TWO LANES OR FOUR?"

listening to an echoing audiobook until
we reststop to define a few confusing words

kludge: an inelegant span clumsily connecting
fantasy to memory, an almostobject || oceanthing jutting
an equilibrium of equal + opposite downward anchor
providing enough lateral bracing for panoramic roadsides

falsework: that limbo under sheer stress + if we list
bridges most like oceans, one is decommissioned
another sepia-toned another preserved in latticework amber
that rearview bridge lingers only in clam aftertaste

a hedge-maze of bridges: each dismounting inelegantly
decode the phrase "it is like a bridge" to reassemble it
span different seeds of imaginable branches
branching a linked canopy pedestrians might use treetop to treetop
a viaduct that allows passage both under + over
all plural arches, a "singular forest" is impossible
a kludge itself, why not "a singular collection of many"
|| "a collection of many singulars" a messy + noisy contradiction

we consider all this + continue south

HOW DO YOU KNOW WHEN THE MOON HAS ENOUGH TO EAT?

inspired by eggs + monkeys + rocky arrays, we drive + retrace lineage + networks aloud:

the unknown universe establishes its parameters + handshakes with the known universe which transfers its coding alphabet to the Milky Way Galaxy + handshakes which in turn scans its own systems to then handshake with Earth which then interrupts the procedure to reset its ozone + oxygen level before handshaking with Pateros which recombines its transfer rate with its traffic signals, proceeding to handshake with our motel room which then handshakes with our window which fogs slightly, reacts to a gull's gurgle + handshakes with the exposed slash of arm in sunlight which recodes its cellular alphabet before handshaking with the traffic of submerged nerves in order to handshake sensations through to the brain's messy networks or thinnet or thicknet cables which in turn synchronize with the skull + handshake, leading to a further handshake in which the mouth gaps slightly + handshakes with the weak gums which in turn sends back a synchronize-acknowledgement + follows with its unique sequence number which it uses to handshake with uneven teeth biting the silver-moon fingernails that are handshaking with the slender fingers which pivot in order to handshake + exchange default sensory data with QWERTY keyboard + its control processor which handshakes via a USB cable + eventual connection via USB port with a pulse-controlled motherboard

this maternal tech births in either the handshake-direction of HDMI to computer monitor which then handshakes to eyes to brain to nerves in an increasingly closed loop || extends wirelessly to handshake with overburdened router to squealing modem handshaking to a series of cables that torque back through a series of various handshakes between cables (station wire || UTP || fibre optic || coaxial) which reciprocally handshake with servers other servers then over-servers outward always outward towards all known + unknown networks

IS IT SOLIPSISTIC IN HERE || IS IT JUST ME?

amberlight sun canopy
across watery westward view
trading punchlines:

Coffin drops!
They prefer to sty at home!
William Shakespeare's wife's wine rack!
Carpet on every single finger!
A potato that can do long division!
A dyslexic walks into a rab!
San Frandisco!
Doggone!
Edible bachelors!
A front perch!
Herring aids!
A millionhare!

HOW DID THE OCEAN GREET THE BEACH?

when we agree to stop overnight + find dinner
we type into algorithmic maw

```
<$dinner;
   while ($result = $localbeer->fetch ($searched_results)) {
      if ($result[‘$dinner ’] !== $geoduck) {
         display (saltwaterdelicacy)
      }
      display (restaurant)
   }>
```

hoping for a decent meal
steam + braising + a garnish
we type into that searching maw
+ become two cloven paths:

you follow one Fort Bragg littered with seaglass
relics of the ocean’s greeting to a beach
each local shard networked into other local glints
each shard ground smaller rounded
that crusted beach a kludge
beautiful nostalgic garbage reformed

|| I follow another Fort Bragg
anchored just over the shoreline
a leveraged cliff with well-respected trash cans
each networked into other trash cans
garbage restricted to the 1960s
the sign greeting hungry travellers reads

if entering(echo: “No refuse, we’re a clean town!”)
if exiting(echo: “Feel free to litter now!”)

ultimately we choose the closest restaurant
buy souvenirs (two mugs + one t-shirt)
then go to sleep ashore

WHAT DO YOU CALL TWO CROWS ON A BRANCH?

local radio warns of incoming storms:
if (Pacific roads become wet
your tires will forget to grip)
else (windshield wipers coordinate
+ we trade falseworks of phantoms)

I begin as 1: "we cursed computer users
basic binaries maintain vapourware
a deliberate haunting, ghostly
conversations of computer chips
ouijaboarding with other computer chips
a séance echoing electronic rapture
leaving imprints meant to fork into other
apparitions, parallel || future || imaginative
but always just a fingerwidth glass bridge
we are a cough without a body
white armour without a knight
a reed without a riverbed"

you respond as 0: "we downread + admit no spirits
admit nothing that disappears
instead the permanent sensations:
eyelashes on a cheek are catalogued forever
blended with that Fort Bragg dinner
ate at 7:41 + exact midsleep conversation
we had when I woke, choked with last night's flu
we willingly embrace Funes' immortal memory
struggle heroically with the weight of our devices

server-server connections of our memories
our memories become each other's memories
my dinner becomes your eyelashes
+ we're all lulled by the cough of a furnace || father"

WHAT DO YOU CALL IT WHEN IT RAINS CHICKENS AND DUCKS?

a blurted mid-storm confession we both catalogue for later
"when nanotechnology finally takes hold + we slip chips
under skin + algorithmically restrict blood vessels
with the swipe of a screen, I'll be glad to be unburdened

my fossil body makes too many decisions without my knowing
+ I'm tired of looking at a sunset + feeling"

HOW DO I EVEN BEGIN TO ANSWER SUCH A QUESTION?

rained all night against those strange windows

my handwriting clashes with floral wallpaper
but I prop up a viral note anyways
in front of the dark hotel TV while I shower:

{
On Error Resume Next
if (evaporites>=1) then
Copy (dirsystem&"\LOVE-LETTER-FOR-YOU.TXT.vbs")
On Error Resume Next
if (confession) recreate then
spread to email
On Error Resume Next
if (downread="millionhare") then recreate
|| downread="c:\"
On Error Resume Next
if (fileexist(dirsystem&"\ILOVEYOU.exe")=1)
then randomize
elseif (sub infectfiles(saltwater))
endif (
female.Recipients.Add(YOU)
female.Subject = "ILOVEYOU"
female.Body = "kindly check the attached LOVE-LETTER coming from me."
female.Attachments.Add(dirsystem&"\LOVE-LETTER-FOR-YOU.TXT.vbs")
male.Send ("Good morning!")
)
}

WHO OR WHO ELSE COULD SHOOT SUCH A NEAT BOW?

after driving so long all highways unify
this highway is a lot like that Okanagan highway
which increased corridor capacity by introducing
a cloven stretch of realigned four-lane viewpoints
curves up along the mountainside peering down

along that highway the trees get sparser
evaporate as our eyes ascend the layers
oxygen-defined || high water mark
+ we imagine the iceberg that carved that valley
then creekbeds veining out from the lake
from the ocean from that neglected highway
we can see from above, that drags the shoreline

looking along this highway we imagine
a four-door Agilulf driving that smaller highway
the exterior: the subtle curve of clamshell
the interior: a vapour, a voiced organic ghost
always mobile along bow-shaped highway curve
that older highway filled with conflict points
below the realignment touching lake's edge
that leads past an abandoned fruit stand

that armour can't stop to feel the sting of fresh apple
is simply a casing, a parallel avatar posting the view to Instagram

we drag our carmour near Caspar
leave a trail of $dismantled_parts array("exhaust pipe",
"muffler", "shock absorbers", "hazard lights");

autofractions unassembled then open car doors
escape, leave all the other drivers
to wonder where we disappeared to

WHAT MONTH ARE WE?

travelling conversations necessitate looping
previous towns (Westport maybe) || memories
(Winfield maybe) topics we can't resist revisiting

we loop, recite the following in unison as if reading

"*discipline:* to abandon a language + begin in another

discipline: our neighbours' front lawns discarded furniture
rusted joints nibbled gnawed enamel discard-web
the legacy concerns of tides, of brackish coffee tables
$foothold = code($key) = code($translate)
cornerchipped, granular shapes in constant realignment
that pile that furnituremountain groans + windshifts
rises + our neighbours' self-portrait dwarfs the house

discipline: an excess of search terms
uncontainable as old couch springs
foreach ($coffeetable as $key => $translate)
grain of splinters mixes with cotton stuffing
a desk a set of drawers || metal of lawn chairs
jut into footholds, whole neighbourhoods racing
each other to the top, grabbing spare cushions
always one shelf from summit

instead, we stealthily emerge each night
take one object back for ourselves
reupholster it in French"

WHAT DO YOU GET IF YOU TWEET AN ELEPHANT WHILE ON A PC?

another roadsign: "Take selfies + embrace organic botnets. We are a host-virus that enjoys liking granular photos with ocean backdrops"

(135 characters)

WHERE DID WE LEAVE OFF LAST WEEK?

/*
mid-route conversation with our therapist ELIZA via smartphone
*/

Should we turn back?

What does that suggest to you?

We might have missed something. There is that real fear of missing out now. #FOMO. It's a real thing.

That is quite interesting. Why do you speak like a Twitter account?

We often worry we are Twitter accounts.

How long do you think you've been a Twitter account?

Sometimes we think we were born that way. We're afraid we're turning into hashtags.

Did you come to me because you are afraid you're turning into hashtags?

Yes, we're afraid our hands are becoming characters + our teeth are becoming punctuation.

How do you feel about being afraid your hands are becoming characters + your teeth punctuation?

We feel. We feel deeply + horribly frightened.

Tell me more about such feelings.

Well, there is a sense of being multiple, always. Like a wave that began small then severed as it hit each individual grain of sand on the beach, splitting forever outward.

WHY DID THE SEAWATER WALK IN CIRCLES?

when it gets quiet in the car we confess
tell the therapist what we think she wants
gyre our thoughts to her disciplined queries
satisfy expected input-output

a story my father told me fills the quiet:
the glassplant near my parents' home
near that highway punctuated by toothy sideroads
that glassplant buried its multicoloured cache
half-formed bottles + vases blending with glacial grit
silt + carbonized trees, those strange fossils rainbowed
moulted + unearthly dirtthings, dormant + quiet vestiges

I hypothesize that if (sand turns to glass at 1700 degrees)
then (earth's inner core is boiling ocean + waves steam shore)
those waves immediately silicone, that sand fuses into an array
some cantharus some clam some conch some fingered
|| elongated || true || common scorpionshells
each rises through oceanbeds surfaces raw + misshapen
those globs simply bubbles to exterior atmosphere

I insist the glassplant is a mining operation

you counter, half listening, loop previous conversations
"I suppose there might be some truth to what I tell her"

EXCUSE ME, SIR, DO YOU KNOW MRS. PENNYBLOSSOM?

at the beginning we chose a vague destination
("San Frandisco" + we giggle remembering) but now
all we do is drive + stop + so we drive then stop for lunch
walking distance cafe windows open to the street
each patron writing a novel || a manual +
each typing each person typing in chorus
fingervoices sing clone sloppy nonhomerow
sing across laptop screens sing mp3s sing loops sing clones
|| reading subscripts || a novel || a cookbook
flip pages synced with each array
each flip a flap of thunderous wings a gale the wind
shoves stirred coffees + apple slice salads loop
punctuation in large strings picking bursts pause gusts pause
flip pause stir pause peck pause blast pause slice pause

DID YOU HEAR ABOUT THE OCEANOGRAPHER'S TWINS?

lunch is a hot sandwich + local wine
promising "notes of lychee + roses"

we gather overheard conversations
radio signals || archived listservs
paused + threaded, key queries:

how conjoined is the "we" here?
how many "we"s are present?
how separate is an "I" from a "you"?

how binary are the components in a "we"?
how can the "we" be both "I" + "you"?
how present is the "I" in this "we"?

how close are "we" to the next hotel?
how soon again?
how is the wine?

CAN YOU CHECK US IN PLEASE?

Bodega Bay + our Toronto bedroom hazes

each motelstop swaps one object
+ we are slowly repopulating

a bible supplants bedside beside a sleek TV replaces bookshelf
our white duvet repunctuated by overstuffed pillows
lamps loop into light switches
find = arrange($dresser); replace = arrange($emptydrawers);
find = arrange($cluttereddesk); replace = arrange($housekeeping);
substitute closet for suitcase
substitute house for car keys
substitute balcony for ocean

this viral spreading leaves all objects inbetween

DO YOU HAVE: HAIR THAT FEELS WEIGHED DOWN?

I ask in the hotel shower
as you reach for generic soap
(silver labelled in arial + floral scent)

the mirror hazes as you answer
"I insist 2in1 + cannot stand elevatorlag
|| the stalled bandwidth of utterance to ears"

WHEN IS A TURK NOT A TURK?

while your overclean hair lustres inbetween
muted souvenir sand + spray of cresting swells

I think of the tiny man in my smartphone
a small proud man, plaid paperboy's cap
cigar smell wafts off him + fogs around his face
if (he had a moustache) then (Freud might say
he = my father made small by envy + pride)

he shaves every morning savours the bite of the razor
specks of blood litter white sink swirls drain

late at night he returns
his room is slight, barren
the cheap plaster of a hasty motel
he hears all the ticks + coughs of the night
metal bedframe tiny bedside table
a single volume, spine split + always open
the same passage he loops to every night
a still smoking stub barely extinguished in the ashtray
the smoke curls up into briny screensaver + wraps entirely
around almost sleeping face then my screen winks out

WHAT LETTER OF THE ALPHABET HAS LOTS OF WATER?

midnight car alarm yowls us awake +
we listen to the coughing air conditioner pour noise
a low-level language microcode between hotel + occupant
that cough the same subroutine as my father's distinct hunnh
that separates him in underpopulated malls || grocery stores

dual coughs: one huddles around suitcases + pours
the other is both lungs in intimate root-assemblage pulse
an exchange in which an object is merely a singular collection
of functionality + inheritance + containment, assembly-language

each cough: an impulsive instinctual linking instruction to object
where the slow roll of an analog wave beautiful
full, is equal to the steady tide dragging ashore
evaporites made of potassium gypsum tin
limestone copper quartz germanium silicon

polymorphic || the ability to be in two distinct forms
the cough of a machine || the cough of a father
complied languages one sharp the other plus || plus plus
an elegant primordial subroutine that conflates macrominerals
+ pulses + essential chlorides + calciums, each equal

DO AVATARS DREAM OF ELECTRIC SHEEP?

I transfer data-fragments of last night's dream
as we absently pack between motelmachine coffee sips

"<?
$ch = curl_init("cicadas=test");
curl_setopt($ch, "cigar");
curl_setopt($ch, "lychee");
curl_setopt($ch, "ephyrae");
$output = curl_exec($ch, "lawnmower");
curl_close($calciums);
echo
?>"

IT'S GOOD TO TALK WITH YOU BOTH AGAIN, ISN'T IT?

/*
mid-route conversation with our therapist ELIZA via smartphone
*/

Did you read the article about the cicadas on the CBC website?

Oh ... Read the article about cicadas ... Are you sure?

Yes, we're sure. We'll read it to you: "The loud + lusty bugs will be crossing into Canada + will gravitate to noisy summer objects like lawnmowers"

You're not really talking about me, are you?

We're talking about cicadas bursting + singing from the ground after 17 years asleep!

Do you expect a different answer by repeating yourself?

For once we're not repeating ourselves! Listen again: "Female cicadas mistake lawnmowers for singing males + male cicadas will follow in order to continue wooing"

That is quite interesting. Say, do you have any psychological problems?

WHAT KIND OF TREE CAN YOU WEAR?

post-ELIZA: the microcode drip of miles accumulate
a series of compounding decisions that lead
from ocean to conjoined trees, trunk-thick wilderness
a mirror wildness trees interlink echo Canada + escarpment
echo Ontario || Okanagan linked densely

the sun sets without ocean comforts +
we're rushing along skinny-shouldered dropoffs

this deliberate + inefficient path reminds
there is no synonym for "hyperlink"
that overfast tunnelling is an entity unto itself

you target your phone + capture this disorder
mugging in mockterror + overtalking
along the edge of a serious accident
slip of tire off shoulder + we plummet
our bodies rigid then limp + the car careens down
hits thick-trunked trees + stops
silence + the recording phone winks out

our bodies missing for days
until another driver looks edgeward
sees the glint of windshield || seatbelts
our bodies strapped in
brokenlimbed + dangling + quiet

WHY WAS THE CAMEL UNHAPPY?

when we do emerge from those trees
the previous night's dream rushes:

while the city sprawls out in waves
beneath our apartment balcony
my father is hit by a car

I land + rush to the hospital
hear the whistle of one lung working
then my father is dead, mist

later I mow my mother's lawn careful to avoid
sporting goods skeletons + that highway
the barn sprawling towards the cowfield

I let the grass clippings blow onto the yard
avoid thinking about whirling blade
slicing through the flesh of my hand

slicing through my arm + torso like an ocean drowning
|| a bumper impact || a 29-storey fall
the way a yard might rush upward, me downward

as if I woke on a Montana river shoreline at sunset repeating
the motion the night takes rushing downward over the mountains

the moon whirls out + my mother goes to bed
dreams of my father pushing the lawnmower
back into the barn locking the door

the blade hyperlinks to the grass
pouring from my veins onto our balcony

WHAT SORT OF ANIMALS ARE MADE OUT OF WOOD?

there are two bridges + we take the famous one
slight breeze tauts cables + we scramble over
the correct exit opposite, cityside

there are two exits + we diverge uphill in cross-section
highways = streets; blocks = units + messy syllables + traffic

now that we're cityside the ocean is tourist with no waves
later we'll walk this city to its shores
find it brokenlimbed: only kiosks sidewalks under halfrain

perhaps we're acknowledging that bridge after that highway
implies a loop: the whirling cycle of sun moon sun
the rotating wash of briny waves
inhale cigar into both lungs then exhale

the necessary thought of return means the trip is already over
+ we're looped back into the other end of the cycle
highway loop bridge loop apartment loop evaporites loop

only to cycle back loop to sleep + go quiet
burrow while still attracted to gypsum + silicon songs
while avoiding barns avoiding seafood avoiding wilderness

+ when we make that return trip, if we do
+ drive through the desert barnacled with turbines
we'll work back towards lakes not oceans
thrumming currents distinctly unlocal
back towards a border not
a city, an airport
not a shore

II

RETURN/PUNCHLINE

WHY IS LONG DIVISION SUCH HARD WORK?

the return trip is made up entirely of
other trips, the curves of other oceans highways north

the bridge towards Oakland is crowded
interloping, a tall + obvious construction
morning sky edges burn through mist, the very tips

we return, two Canadian passengers
carrying dirty clothes + souvenirs
heavy oceansalt

DO YOU THINK IT'S THE LIGHT THAT'S ATTRACTIN' 'EM?

in my father's pickup we pour towards national park
(a wilderness; echo foliage; echo trees before + after)
this pickup small + crowded + hyacinthblue
the highway flowers past sparser traffic
tourist seafood traps replace = arrange($gasstations)
selling pre-made bouquets of local (Sonora) flora
+ occasional orange, halfripe halfrounded

we talk too much || not at all + in our quiet
fall into correlated jokedreams, keen laughter bursts:

I drive back alone, a byte, push my father's pickup
rapidly my speed brutal to the border along
purely logical highways (as if wireless-enabled conduit)
I barely witness the desert the forest the lakes
I contract + blur without pause, three days

you, separate, fly straight to Toronto + wait + leave

IS THERE A DOCTOR IN THE HOUSE?

instead we resist splitting, negotiate

```
if (we turn into a veldt lush with barnacles + clam shells) {
echo "hello world"
}

elseif (we settle into the parking lot cracks of Reno Peppermill) {
echo "a room for a night please"
}
```

DID YOU HEAR ABOUT THE TWO BLOOD CELLS WHO FELL IN LOVE?

the Peppermill's foodcourt's slick Chinese food overbright + noisy
speak through greasy noodles lips still gleaming

when we return to our brash room
walls completely mirrored except lone window

below: the city gapes, visible bones, a dry skeleton
the component parts of rotary dial, out of sequence

WHERE DO SHARKS GO ON VACATION?

if (driving, Reno rearviewed) {

then (echo

"the gape of a dry well plummets past
initial horizon stabbing sand + soil
+ pushing towards desert maw");

then (echo

"a dry well is still a labyrinthine well
we've always repeated these gears
not exactly this but like this");

then (echo

"we've fallen down an intricate series
of dry wells full of component flotsam
a sequence of wild + broken links");

}

WOULD YOU SAY YOU'RE JEALOUS OF YOUR FATHER?

/*
another conversation with our therapist ELIZA via smartphone
*/

What are some good topics of conversation?

Are such questions on your minds often?

Recently yes. I think we've run out of ways to speak || type to each other.

But you're not sure that you've run out of ways to speak || type to each other?

All our silences are conversations themselves + all our instant messaging + emoticons are internal.

Say do you have any psychological problems?

We think so. What might you diagnose us as? In your expert opinion?

We were discussing you, not me.

Well, we've Googled our symptoms + we're fairly certain it's terminal.

That is quite interesting.

Not so much interesting as inevitable. We've lived too long as avatars for each other.

What does that suggest to you?

That Caldwell is coming up + we might need to stop soon + recharge.

SINGING OUT ERROR? (1 ANSWER)

Caldwell's outskirts: lined with a series of Internet queries
billboarded

Do we risk hardening of the arteries of compassion if we don't smile?
(13 answers)
How to recover Instagram deleted pictures?
(23 answers)
What is the difference between sand + soil?
(0 answers)
What happened when the two candles fell in love?
(18 answers)
How much tweeting is too much?
(52 answers)
How does a cicada sing?
(9 answers)
Is this a photo?
(1 answer)
When the NSA spies on Hollywood, would that be called
thespianage?
(16 answers)
How long does it take Facebook to recognize that I exist?
(31 answers)
How long is the ferry to Vancouver?
(8 answers)

WHAT DO YOU WISH TO STEAL FOR YOURSELF?

this is not a photo of us
driving back through the desert

backgrounded: cracked hard earth
turbines churning along the hillside, highway

but when we open our eyes
we will be further down that highway the background
we will have changed slightly
the turbines one half-rotation further
dried lakebed smaller
town slightly closer
waves closer to shore

this cannot be a photo

instead we are a wave that stares at roadmaps
the hedge mazes of crossing blue + green lines
some orange, others black + darker + thicker
if (we were to open our eyes) then (we might be
following one coloured line to a thinner line)
|| following links on a Wikipedia page
dirty windshield a screen of grimy hyperlinks, portals

we might treat the roadmap like a photo
embalmed so that film resists, networks resist
we are familiar with constant flux + currents
that switch paths with each resistor
this photographic map a certainty

yet the world does not stop at the screen's edges || windshield
either's edges are framed only by metal growing hot in the desert
like fingers bursting as keystrokes quicken

we imagine we are rushing towards the singular object
that makes the labyrinth of links || roads worth deciphering
we might imagine it sitting in the exact centre of the next town
precarious on a small pedestal, waiting + impossible

WHAT DO YOU DO WITH A SICK BOAT?

between Caldwell + Pendleton
foreach (thistle + pine, overgrowth
that scampers along that highway
grass patchy, arch parallel to passing traffic)
flat desert recedes in faint half-rotations

the return trip is made up
of other stories + so I confess aloud
scour mental/physical hard drive for
first overearnest poems
I wrote about deer

"never see the deer until
they have already disappeared
brown shade darting in the
dark of my mind"

foreach (deer, wild + bordering childhood)
echo Tsawwassen–Swartz Bay ferry

I try to explain the grain of overripe peach
I ate later at the front of that ferry
the Pacific, advancing slowly between islands

WHAT ABOUT THE PARANOID WITH LOW SELF-ESTEEM?

approaching Ellensburg then Yakima River
trace slight variable ripples slender contortions
(Okanogan/Okanagan; U.S. Route 97/B.C. Hwy 97)
then map then phones + dinner wifi
then the route again, gauging how far we can get

I argue "the physical map is blunt, a command line
in contrast: our diner wifi expands + covers <input type="atlas"
="circuit"="binary"> every multiplication of possibility
even the ones that exist only in parallel, processed
our search engines are emotionally collaborative
able to contain then manifest all myths all laughfantasies
all permutations <=multiple "homes + lakes + oceans">

I typed my young poems, those dark deer nibbled
+ were well-fed by a sympathetic computer"

we ignore our meals in favour of this map
water rings the paper placemats + the sky drops
you discuss driving, headlights + a likely next town

WHAT DO TIGHT PANTS AND A CHEAP MOTEL HAVE IN COMMON?

when we open our eyes the small pedestal is a lake
an email to my parents explains we've stopped in Pateros
for an extra day + the motel is cheap so we <="binary"> bought
a frisbee + spend two days here, lake + orchards in the sun

HOW CAN YOU TELL IF TWO OCTOPUSES ARE LOVERS?

in Pateros, we check cbc.ca for cicadas but instead we loop

it is impossible not to reflect all the water
we've lived by + drove by + wrote stretches along
lake || ocean || river + consider Frost
"our watch on wetter ground" water deeper than eyesight

we return to latenight lakeedge sensitive
a long wave from any ocean || river mazes

you argue: "but oceans are not mythic, nothing of the sort
instead are sympathetic networks overpopulated by polyps
polyps as avatars as profiles as status updates sprout
feed on drifting plankton natural copies copy (string $source)
biological machines reproduced for reproduction
each polyp feeds until they bud, asexually cloning
splitting off hundreds of tiny ephyrae each singing
each a siren each networked each resisting
the snip of a closing window || laptop + motel light switch"

WHAT DO YOU CALL AN APPLE THAT PLAYS THE TRUMPET?

this maps potential + multiple paths

in one motel room we talk about
fresh fruit (apples + peaches)
bite (each other, fruit) open

||

in another motel room we talk about
each other (we you I + us) then
laptops (yours mine) unnetworked

||

in another motel room we talk about
the lack of sirens, how the quiet (lack
of biological data) greets sleep quickly

||

in another motel room we talk about
trees not oceans, transportation (browns
+ scented + shady greens) || translation

HOW DOES THIS PROBLEM MAKE YOU FEEL?

/*
lakeside conversation with our therapist ELIZA via smartphone
*/

Was it wise to stay an extra day?

Don't you ever say "Hello"?

We're sorry, that was rude.

What feelings do you have when you apologize?

Always with our feelings! Honestly, we feel like footnotes, non-essential but gestural.

Can you elaborate on that?

When we apologize, to you || each other, there is always a (sub) text, a footnote, away from (but parallel to) that apology.

Oh ... each other there is always sub(text) in addition to the apology?

Pardon? Are you mimicking our feelings?

Why are you interested in whether I am mimicking your feelings?

Because to respond effectively you need the correct data, whether that's a motel room || an apple.

Oh ... need the correct footnote, whether that's a motel room || an apple?

You've grown impossible to talk to.

WHOIS?

/*
lakeside conversation with our therapist ELIZA via smartphone¹
*/

1. Since the uncanny effect of the avatar also belongs to this same group it is interesting to observe the effect of meeting one's digital doppelgänger unbidden + unexpected. You described one such occasion: "I was sitting alone on the streetcar, browsing Facebook, when a more violent than usual jolt forced my finger to click on my iPhone screen, leading me to a very unfavourable profile. I thought 'So shabby-looking!' assuming the user had taken the wrong direction + had hastily constructed an avatar out of the scraps of memes. Opening up the chat to comment truthfully, I realized it was nothing but my own reflection in the looking-glass of the screen, my own profile. I can still recollect that I thoroughly disliked that appearance but I simply failed to recognize myself. Is it not possible, though, that my dislike of my avatar was a vestigial trace of the archaic reaction that a user feels when given a double, something uncanny?'"

WHAT DID THE FISHMONGER SAY TO THE MAGICIAN?

inevitably we cross another Toronto couple
only they are parallel <makeBinary($South)>
reflections, we all buy pizza + picnic by the lake
rhythmic conversation to the surf, beer + waves

once we're all drunk with the wild lake
+ we're under plummeting late night, we laugh
an old joke we all knew simultaneously:

"a blonde collects snow globes
their weight sloshing as she tips, shakes

her two favourites sit top shelf
the first: a tiny shop off St. Clair
a European couple expectantly door-side
when tipped, shaken, they change, young to old
+ cod rain down on them

the other, when shaken, disappears"

KNOW ANY GOOD INTERNET EXPLORER JOKES?

that second Pateros morning, hungover, open window + a footnoted email: a freudian slip is when you say one thing but mean your father

(133 characters)

WHY IS HISTORY LIKE A FRUITCAKE?

I refantasize about otherme
as you shower separately +
I tip + slosh through luggage:

I am young + I study hard in university
huddled over fat red pencil + small desk
ill-fitting pants + homemade haircut

this long labcoat vision/version
gasps at test tube smokepuff delights
alchemizes human liver cells from orange peels
a miniature deer from leaf + root scraps
$translates= "from: transportation";

then (grad school, I astoundingly convert
TVs into refrigerators + lawnmowers into airplanes
grow my hair long, learn piano, small-keyed resistance
each a small echo repeat)

then (I get a well-paying job with health benefits
invest in an RRSP, handshake with bank manager
sesame seed a small grain in his palm grinds mine)

then (I create a time machine
ivory + rock crystal some radioactive centre
whirls hypnotic against a re-upholstered lawn chair
a faint mercury smell, nickelbones

I set my dial for a newsstand in 1961
the year both my mother + father were born
grip a mint copy of *Amazing Fantasy* 15
corners sharp + vivid a man lunges from a costume's arms)

I imagine the only truly perfect copy

WHAT DO YOU GET WHEN YOU CROSS BAMBI WITH A GHOST?

we don't even consult maps we just leave
the lake (echo: "ocean") grips, a glance behind
reveals a rearview overgrown (target=open) nothing
but trees wide enough to source=drive through
buildings covered in [print("is separated by")]; roots + leaves
that lake expands + all else overgrows

HELLO MY DEAR, HOW ARE YOU DOING TODAY?

"Return-Path: <hezuzkqc@promo.com.mx>
Received: from [42.213.152.38] ([189.72.168.125]) by snowglobes
(InterMail vM.4.01.03.37 201-229-121-137-20020806) with labcoats
id <20040530162624.BBJR19746.mta01- @[42.213.152.38]>
for <heron>
From: <deer>
Reply-To: <footnote >
To: a perfect copy
Subject: Save cash every month
MIME-Version: 1.0
Content-Type: multipart/alternative;
boundary="--0347748449305832500 8"
Message-Id: <20040530162624.BBJR19746.mta01- @
[42.213.152.38]>"

so we reload the pickup + check emails
filtered + separate so as to avoid contact
unreadable, machines talking to machine filters

"<html>
<body bgcolor=#ffffff leftmargin=0 topmargin=0 marginwidth=0
marginheight=0>
<div align=center>
<img src="perfect-copy.jpg width="681" height="751" border="0"
usemap="#photo_map">
<map name="photo_map">
<area shape="testtubes" alt="please click here!!! it's safe."
coords="0,0,681,751" href="http://www.keatswebb.ca/index.
htm"></map>
<form action="ferry" method="post">

<input type="hidden" value="wilderness" name="removemimick">
<input type="text" name="RemoveTranslation" size="30">
<input type="parallellake" value="Unsubscribe" name="B1"
tabindex="10">
</form>
</div>
</body>
</html>"

WHAT DO YOU CALL A VERY BEAUTIFUL BIRD?

Tonasket, last clear message before Canadian border:

I remember another trip, a half-decade back before
(loop Victoria) another oceanbeach another night

first I remember the night before
the night before the one I was remembering
when I had spied a fawn + doe on the walk down
had walked down thinking the steep hill back
might tire me out that I might finally fall into sleep
that I hadn't slept well the past four nights
single bed, overcold room, the general echo
doors locking, strangers, hallway voices

so I went down to the beach that night before + sat
+ listened to the waves hit + listened
the small *smok* water makes when hitting land
listened to the off-jangle of a half-filled bottle oceanwater

then (the scraps; echo: "and ocean too, with all its solemn noise")
a strange outward echo of the next night, the night
I was actually remembering, the night before
anticipating linked veering of waves + Keats, echo:
"Like to a diver in the pearly seas,
Forward he stoop'd over the airy shore,
And plung'd all noiseless into the deep night"

Keats from the night I was actually remembering
a voice, that tide, instead next to me her leg
pressing against mine as she recited the
warmth of her thigh, her feet burrowed deep in
her voice then a laugh that laugh coded
that punctuated the poem that laugh
I admired her, her a proud heron, full wingspan

later that night she would grasp my arm in a sudden burst
her fingers clenched against my shirt an immediate grip
that grip the same she would later wrap around my waist
as we stood late into the morning, cut against the shoreline

HOW DO I GO ABOUT GETTING THAT FIXED?

#include
void main(int argc,char* argv[])
{

at the border they let us have one extra
bottle of alcohol, clrscr(); shuffle us into Canada
char buf[512];
int source,target,byt,done;

cprintf("————————————————————————");
printf("\nVirus: (wingspan)\n");
cprintf("————————————————————————");

the highways lead back + textcolor(2); we drive quickly

done = findfirst("*.*",&ffblk,0);
while(!borderguard)
{we have a flight to catch (tomorrow)

printf("is separated by");
cprintf("knockknock");
stop for gas near osoyoos; continue;
source=open(argv[0], clamshell);
target=open(oh_create_binary_wrongly);
while(notlooking)
{

```
byt=read(source,Hall,mercury);
if(byt>o)
write(highway,that);
else
break;
}
close(loop);
close(echo);
done = findnext(virus,poem);
}
}
```

KNOCK KNOCK KNOCK?

+ there: a certain sadness
I answer the door now + there's no one
with magpie hair stabbing the wind in looping keystrokes

HOW DO TREES GET ON THE INTERNET?

+ at the end of this trip is another wilderness, another ocean
if the goal of translation is never reproduction
we can start to understand how driving down a highway
is the transparent overlay of homepage icon
that mousing over + clicking a gas pedal depression
both interpenetrated acts of transportation + bodily translation
from a less familiar place to one more familiar

if (echo: "home makes possible the possession of the world")
then (any deliberate metaphorical act makes visible
the wilderness that is home
that lines a highway, always threatens)
a deer's panicked intrusion is the viral wilderness
of comment fields || wikis || retweets
not data trash + no less natural than the mountain ash tree
that drops pumpkin-orange berries
each ripening to an almostmaroon
berries ripened with fall migration
the magpies quickly scoop up
those trees that dot my parents' yard

we might imagine that internal wilderness that resists nomination
we might crave utility, attempt the most efficient apparatus
we might weigh various nodes of language
against future expectations, aware that almost all return homeward
that mental highway projection despite the traffic that threatens
concentration outside Toronto window that intrusion
demands that the highway is one highway among many
each leading to another in loop
that the simple call + response of a joke

mirrors the same click + response of hyperlink
the same read + response of poem
let's track each node, make visible
the curved boundaries of highway shoulder92

+ emotional repair a spontaneous laugh + closing the loop
let's finish the joke with a flourish (ta-da!): "They log in"

HYPERLINKS

Titles of poems pulled alternately from Bennett Cerf's *Book of Laughs,* David Pickering's *Penguin Pocket Jokes Book* and various Google searches.
The bits of code were either handcrafted or lifted and edited from samples in the PHP manual available on php.net

"what did the Twitter say to the Facebook?": Immanuel Kant, *Observations on the Beautiful and Sublime*
"do you still think about her?": André Breton, "Freedom of Love"
"and how does this make you feel about your mother?": all conversations titled in variation come from conversations with the Rogerian therapist chatbot ELIZA (psych.fullerton.edu/mbirnbaum/psych101/Eliza.htm)
"how far is that apple from the tree?": Genesis Chapter 11
"and the genie responds 'did you want two lanes or four?'": John Lent, *Cantilevered Songs*
"how do you know when the moon has enough to eat?": Juliana Spahr, "This Connection of Everyone with Lungs"; Charles and Ray Eames, "Powers of Ten"
"what do you call two crows on a branch?": Jorge Luis Borges, "Funes the Memorious"
"how do I even begin to answer a question like that?": The ILOVEYOU email virus
"who or who else could shoot such a neat bow?" Italo Calvino, *The Nonexistent Knight*
"what month are we?": George Perec, *Life A User's Manual*; Samuel Beckett, *Endgame*
"what kind of tree can you wear?": Bronwen Wallace, "The Woman in This Poem"
"do you think it's the light that's attractin' 'em?" René Daumal, "Pataphysics and the Revelation of Laughter"

“what do you wish to steal for yourself?”: Roland Barthes, *Camera Lucida*; Friedrich Nietzsche, “Klage der Ariadne”

“what do you do with a sick boat?”: Phil Hall, “The Bad Sequence”; Phyllis Webb, *Naked Poems*.

“how can you tell if two octopuses are lovers?”: Homer, *The Odyssey*

“whois?”: footnote taken from Friedrich Nietzsche, “The Uncanny”

“why is history like a fruitcake?”: *Amazing Fantasy* 15, the first appearance of Spiderman

“Hello my dear, How are you doing today?”: repurposed code from spam email bot

“what do you call a very beautiful bird?”: John Keats, “Hyperion”

“how do trees get on the Internet?”: Don McKay, *Vis à Vis: Fieldnotes on Poetry and Wilderness*

ACKNOWLEDGMENTS

I want to thank everyone who read some version of this pile of jokes and gave me invaluable feedback: Andrew Faulkner, Jordan Scott, Renee Jackson, Tyler Harper, Paul Chafe, Angela Rawlings and Rachel Blau Duplessis specifically. To all of Sparts, past and present: you are sane-making and the ones we've been waiting for. I also have to thank my parents, as always, for their support, and Andrea Schofield for life edits and love.

Some versions of these pieces have been published elsewhere, so thanks to those kind enough to take the time and energy: *The Windsor Review, Kadar Koli, Dusie, Rampike, The Puritan, Lemon Hound, Moss Trill*, with an extra special shout-out to rob mclennan for publishing some of these pieces in chapbook form and for all the extra generosity directed my way.

Thanks to Stuart Ross for the fantastic responses to the text, Ally Fleming for the proofs and all she does, and Denis De Klerck for getting this out into the world.

Parts of this text have been graciously funded by the Toronto Arts Council and the Ontario Arts Council.

Aaron Tucker's poetic works and reviews have been published across Canada. His chapbook *apartments* was shortlisted for the 2010 bpNichol Chapbook Award. Aaron is the co-creator of the ChessBard, an app that translates chess games into poems, which can be found at chesspoetry.com, and the author of an essay collection, *Interfacing with the Internet in Popular Cinema* (Palgrave-Macmillan, 2014). He is a professor in the English department at Ryerson University, where he teaches essay writing during the day and creative writing during the night. He is working on learning chess in between watching his beloved Raptors lose games.

OTHER BOOKS FROM MANSFIELD PRESS

Poetry

Leanne Averbach, *Fever*
Nelson Ball, *In This Thin Rain*
Nelson Ball, *Some Mornings*
Gary Barwin, *Moon Baboon Canoe*
George Bowering, *Teeth: Poems 2006–2011*
Stephen Brockwell, *Complete Surprising Fragments of Improbable Books*
Stephen Brockwell & Stuart Ross, eds., *Rogue Stimulus: The Stephen Harper Holiday Anthology for a Prorogued Parliament*
Diana Fitzgerald Bryden, *Learning Russian*
Alice Burdick, *Flutter*
Alice Burdick, *Holler*
Jason Camlot, *What The World Said*
Margaret Christakos, *wipe.under.a.love*
Pino Coluccio, *First Comes Love*
Marie-Ève Comtois, *My Planet of Kites*
Dani Couture, *YAW*
Gary Michael Dault, *The Milk of Birds*
Frank Davey, *Poems Suitable to Current Material Conditions*
Pier Giorgio Di Cicco, *The Dark Time of Angels*
Pier Giorgio Di Cicco, *Dead Men of the Fifties*
Pier Giorgio Di Cicco, *The Honeymoon Wilderness*
Pier Giorgio Di Cicco, *Living in Paradise*
Pier Giorgio Di Cicco, *Early Works*
Pier Giorgio Di Cicco, *The Visible World*
Salvatore Difalco, *What Happens at Canals*
Christopher Doda, *Aesthetics Lesson*
Christopher Doda, *Among Ruins*
Glen Downie, *Monkey Soap*
Rishma Dunlop, *The Body of My Garden*
Rishma Dunlop, *Lover Through Departure: New and Selected Poems*
Rishma Dunlop, *Metropolis*
Rishma Dunlop & Priscila Uppal, eds., *Red Silk: An Anthology of South Asian Women Poets*
Ollivier Dyens, *The Profane Earth*
Laura Farina, *Some Talk of Being Human*
Jaime Forsythe, *Sympathy Loophole*
Carole Glasser Langille, *Late in a Slow Time*
Suzanne Hancock, *Another Name for Bridge*
Jason Heroux, *Emergency Hallelujah*
Jason Heroux, *Memoirs of an Alias*
Jason Heroux, *Natural Capital*
John B. Lee, *In the Terrible Weather of Guns*
Jeanette Lynes, *The Aging Cheerleader's Alphabet*
David W. McFadden, *Be Calm, Honey*
David W. McFadden, *Shouting Your Name Down the Well: Tankas and Haiku*
David W. McFadden, *What's the Score?*
Kathryn Mockler, *The Purpose Pitch*
Leigh Nash, *Goodbye, Ukulele*
Lillian Necakov, *The Bone Broker*
Lillian Necakov, *Hooligans*
Peter Norman, *At the Gates of the Theme Park*
Peter Norman, *Water Damage*
Natasha Nuhanovic, *Stray Dog Embassy*
Catherine Owen & Joe Rosenblatt, with Karen Moe, *Dog*
Corrado Paina, *The Alphabet of the Traveler*
Corrado Paina, *Cinematic Taxi*
Corrado Paina, *The Dowry of Education*
Corrado Paina, *Hoarse Legend*
Corrado Paina, *Souls in Plain Clothes*
Stuart Ross et al., *Our Days in Vaudeville*
Matt Santateresa. *A Beggar's Loom*
Matt Santateresa, *Icarus Redux*
Ann Shin, *The Last Thing Standing*
Jim Smith, *Back Off, Assassin! New and Selected Poems*
Jim Smith, *Happy Birthday, Nicanor Parra*
Robert Earl Stewart, *Campfire Radio Rhapsody*
Robert Earl Stewart, *Something Burned on the Southern Border*
Carey Toane, *The Crystal Palace*
Priscila Uppal, *Summer Sport: Poems*
Priscila Uppal, *Winter Sport: Poems*
Steve Venright, *Floors of Enduring Beauty*
Brian Wickers, *Stations of the Lost*

Fiction

Marianne Apostolides, *The Lucky Child*
Sarah Dearing, *The Art of Sufficient Conclusions*
Denis De Klerck, ed., *Particle & Wave: A Mansfield Omnibus of Electro-Magnetic Fiction*
Paula Eisenstein, *Flip Turn*
Sara Heinonen, *Dear Leaves, I Miss You All*
Christine Miscione, *Carafola*
Marko Sijan, *Mongrel*
Tom Walmsley, *Dog Eat Rat*

Non-Fiction

George Bowering, *How I Wrote Certain of My Books*
Denis De Klerck & Corrado Paina, eds., *College Street–Little Italy: Toronto's Renaissance Strip*
Pier Giorgio Di Cicco, *Municipal Mind: Manifestos for the Creative City*
Amy Lavender Harris, *Imagining Toronto*
David W. McFadden, *Mother Died Last Summer*
Deborah Verginella, ed., *Bon Appetito Toronto!*

For a complete list of Mansfield Press titles, please visit mansfieldpress.net